Every step you take brings you closer to the strength and peace you deserve.

MY BEST KEPT SECRET

A WORKBOOK

RECLAIM YOUR BODY AND SOUL

HEALING FROM TRAUMA AND FINDING EMPOWERMENT

BY CHIOMA CHIME

Disclaimer:

Please note that this workbook is not intended as a substitute for professional medical, psychological, or clinical advice. The exercises and reflections shared here are based on my personal experience and the tools that helped me along my journey. Healing is deeply individual, and I encourage you to seek professional support if needed. This workbook is simply a resource to assist you in your own personal healing process.

Publisher Disclaimer:

The publisher of this story hereby declares that it is not responsible for the content, views, opinions, or any other material expressed within the story. The story's content solely belongs to the author, and any claims, statements, or information provided within the narrative are the author's sole responsibility. The publisher does not endorse or guarantee the accuracy, validity, or completeness of the story's content, and disclaims any liability for any harm, loss, or inconvenience caused by the story's content or its interpretation.

Published in United States of America 10 9 8 7 6 5 4 3 2 1

VMH™ Publishing

MY BEST KEPT SECRET

A WORKBOOK

RECLAIM YOUR BODY AND SOUL

HEALING FROM TRAUMA AND FINDING EMPOWERMENT

Disclaimer:

Please note that this workbook is not intended as a substitute for professional medical, psychological, or clinical advice. The exercises and reflections shared here are based on my personal experience and the tools that helped me along my journey. Healing is deeply individual, and I encourage you to seek professional support if needed. This workbook is simply a resource to assist you in your own personal healing process.

Table of Contents

Objective: To create a safe space for understanding the emotional and physical impact of violations.

- Opening Reflection
- Exercise 1: Mapping Your Trauma
- Reflection & Journaling Prompts

Objective: To understand the effects of violations and how they manifest in your emotions, thoughts, and behaviors.

- Opening Reflection
- Exercise 2: Identifying Patterns
- Reflection & Journaling Prompts

Objective: To explore the self-blame that often accompanies trauma and offer ways to let it go.

- Opening Reflection
- Exercise 3: Challenging Self-Blame
- Reflection & Journaling Prompts

Objective: To reconnect with your body through small, manageable steps toward healing.

- Opening Reflection
- Exercise 4: Mindful Breathing and Grounding
- Reflection & Journaling Prompts

Objective: To reflect on your progress and acknowledge how far you've come.

- Reflection and Final Thoughts

Preface

This workbook is a collection of the tools and reflections that have helped me through my own healing journey. While I can't promise that everything here will work the same way for you, I truly believe these practices can help if you're ready to dive in and start reclaiming your power. I'm not a professional therapist, just someone who has been there, and I want to share what's helped me. The goal is to give you space to explore and heal in your own way, at your own pace. Healing isn't linear, and there's no one right way to do it.

So, let's take this journey together, one step at a time.

Introduction

In *My Best Kept Secret* memoir, I shared my deeply personal journey of surviving violations by people I should have been able to trust. These violations—emotional, psychological, and sexual—leave behind scars that, while not always visible, are profoundly felt. For many survivors, the emotional and psychological wounds can be as painful, if not more so, than what is seen on the surface. Fear, shame, guilt, and confusion can cloud your thoughts, affecting how you experience the world long after the traumatic events have passed.

Healing from trauma is a process—a deeply individual one. It isn't quick, nor is it always a straight line. It's about rediscovering your worth, your voice, and your ability to feel safe again in a world that may have felt threatening or uncertain for far too long. But the truth is, healing is possible. And while you may have lived through immense pain, you are not defined by your past. You are defined by your courage, your resilience, and your commitment to reclaiming your life.

This workbook is a tool to help you along that journey. It's here to support you, guiding you step by step toward healing, empowerment, and reclaiming your sense of self. Please remember, however, that this workbook isn't a substitute for professional support. The exercises, prompts, and reflections I share come from my own experiences and the tools that helped me heal. They're meant to offer encouragement, but not to replace the work you may do with a therapist or other professional.

Each chapter in this workbook addresses different aspects of trauma recovery, starting with acknowledging your experience and moving toward a future full of hope, strength, and possibility. You'll be invited to reflect, journal, and engage in exercises designed to help you reconnect with your inner self. These activities will encourage you to identify emotional patterns tied to your trauma, challenge limiting beliefs, and take back control over your life.

There's no rush in this process. Healing happens in its own time, and every small step you take is progress. This workbook is meant to create a safe, supportive space for you to explore your feelings and experiences, and to envision your future. As you work through the exercises, I hope you'll reconnect with parts of yourself that may have been hidden or forgotten under the weight of your pain.

Above all, remember: you are not alone. Countless others are walking a similar path, and you are supported by a community of people who understand. You have the power to heal, to grow, and to reclaim your life. This workbook is just one step in that process—a tool to help you move forward. My hope is that by the end of this journey, you'll feel more empowered, more compassionate toward yourself, and more confident in your ability to create a future filled with peace, joy, and resilience.

This is your journey. You are worthy of love, respect, and healing.

With love, compassion, and belief in your strength,

Chioma Chime

CHAPTER 1

UNDERSTANDING YOUR TRAUMA

CHAPTER OBJECTIVE

To create a safe space for understanding the emotional and physical impact of violations.

Healing starts when we acknowledge what's happened to us. Trauma—whether emotional, physical, or sexual—affects how we feel, how we think, and how we move through life. This chapter is about gently looking at those experiences, recognizing how they've shaped us, but also realizing they don't define us.

Opening Reflection

Your trauma is real, and it's okay if it feels overwhelming. It's okay if you're scared to face it. But know this: you are strong, and you have the power to start healing right now. Take a moment to think about the events that have really affected you. These experiences have shaped how you see yourself and the world around you, but they don't have to control your future.

Exercise 1: Mapping Your Trauma

Think about the key events in your life that have shaped who you are today. Write about them—what happened? How did it feel at the time?

____

____

____

____

____

____

____

____

____

____

____

____

____

____

____

____

____

____

Prompt: What emotions do you associate with these experiences?

____

____

____

Reflection Prompt: How has trauma affected how you see and feel about your body?

____

____

Journaling Prompt: Write about one moment that still impacts you. What thoughts, emotions, and physical sensations come up when you think about it?

CHAPTER 2

THE IMPACT OF VIOLATIONS

CHAPTER OBJECTIVE

To understand how violations affect your emotions, thoughts, and behaviors.

Trauma leaves its mark not just on our emotions, but also in the way we react to situations. Violations can create patterns of fear, avoidance, or hypervigilance. This chapter will help you start to notice these patterns, so you can begin to change them, bit by bit.

Opening Reflection

Trauma messes with our ability to trust—ourselves, other people, even the world. But healing starts when we see those patterns and choose to change them, even if it's just one small step at a time.

Exercise 2: Identifying Patterns

Think about any behaviors or habits you've picked up since your trauma. Do you avoid certain places, people, or situations? Are there times when you just don't feel safe, even when there's no real danger?

____

____

____

____

____

____

____

____

____

____

____

____

____

____

____

____

____

____

____

____

Prompt: How do you react when you feel threatened or unsafe?

____

____

____

____

____

____

____

____

____

____

____

____

____

____

____

____

Reflection Prompt: How does your body feel when you're anxious or scared?

____

____

____

____

____

____

____

____

____

____

____

Journaling Prompt: Write about a time you felt fear in a situation that should have been safe. What triggered it? What did you feel physically in that moment?

CHAPTER 3

THE SELF-BLAME TRAP

CHAPTER OBJECTIVE

To challenge the self-blame that often comes with trauma and learn how to let it go.

We often carry guilt that isn't ours to carry. In this chapter, we'll work on recognizing those harmful thoughts and learning to replace them with kindness and self-compassion.

Opening Reflection

It's easy to fall into the "I must've done something wrong" mindset after trauma. But you didn't cause what happened to you. You were a victim, not the cause. In this chapter, we'll look at how to let go of self-blame and replace it with the love and understanding you deserve.

Exercise 3: Challenging Self-Blame

Write down any self-blame thoughts that come up when you think about your trauma. Are they true? Or are they just rooted in shame and guilt? Try to reframe them with love and compassion.

Prompt: What beliefs about yourself do you carry because of your trauma? How can you shift them to be more compassionate?

____
____
____
____
____
____
____
____
____
____
____
____
____
____

Reflection Prompt: How can you start to let go of the guilt and shame you're holding onto?

____
____
____
____
____
____
____
____
____
____
____
____
____
____
____
____
____

Journaling Prompt: Write a letter to yourself as if you were your own best friend. What would you say to support and encourage yourself through this process?

CHAPTER 4

RECLAIMING YOUR BODY

CHAPTER OBJECTIVE

To reconnect with your body, step by step, and start healing.

After trauma, it's common to feel disconnected from our bodies. But your body has been with you through it all. Reconnecting with it is one of the first steps to healing.

Opening Reflection

Your body isn't the enemy. It's your home, the vessel that's held you through every hard moment. Reclaiming it means rediscovering the strength and beauty it holds.

Exercise 4: Mindful Breathing and Grounding

Try some deep breathing exercises to calm your nervous system. With every breath, focus on filling your body with healing energy.

Prompt: What do you notice when you breathe deeply?

____

____

____

____

____

____

____

____

____

____

____

____

Reflection Prompt: How do you feel about your body right now? What parts of it can you appreciate for their strength and resilience?

____

____

____

____

____

____

____

____

____

____

____

____

Journaling Prompt: Write a letter of gratitude to your body for everything it's done for you, for carrying you through every difficult moment.

CHAPTER 5

REBUILDING TRUST AND SAFETY

CHAPTER OBJECTIVE

To rebuild trust in yourself and others and create a sense of safety in your life.

After trauma, trusting yourself and others can feel impossible. But trust is something we can slowly rebuild—starting with trusting ourselves again. In this chapter, we'll talk about setting boundaries and learning how to create a safer environment for yourself.

Opening Reflection

Rebuilding trust, especially after betrayal, starts with learning to trust yourself and your instincts again. It also means setting boundaries with others so you can feel safe.

Exercise 5: Building Safety

Think about people, places, and activities that make you feel safe. Start to include more of them in your routine.

Prompt: What boundaries can you set with others that will help you feel safer?

Reflection Prompt: How do you react when you feel unsafe or threatened?

Journaling Prompt: Describe a time when you felt truly safe. What was going on around you that made you feel secure?

CHAPTER 6

MOVING TOWARD EMPOWERMENT

CHAPTER OBJECTIVE

To take small, intentional steps toward reclaiming your power.

Healing is a journey—sometimes slow, sometimes fast, but always forward. This chapter will help you take small steps to rebuild your confidence and inner strength.

Opening Reflection

Empowerment doesn't happen overnight. It's built one step at a time— through small acts of courage, self-care, and self-compassion. Every step, no matter how small, is a victory in reclaiming your power.

Exercise 6: Affirmations for Empowerment

Write a list of affirmations that inspire self-love and strength. Repeat them daily, letting the words sink into your heart.

Examples:

"I am worthy of love and respect."
"My body is mine to cherish and protect."
"I am healing, and I am strong."

____

____

____

____

____

____

____

____

____

____

____

____

____

____

____

____

____

Prompt: How do you feel when you say these affirmations out loud?

Reflection Prompt: What does empowerment look like for you right now?

Journaling Prompt: Write about a time you did something for yourself that made you feel proud and empowered.

CHAPTER 7

JOURNALING AND RELEASING THE PAST

CHAPTER OBJECTIVE

To use journaling as a tool to release pain and reclaim your power.

Writing can be one of the most powerful ways to let go of the emotions we carry. In this chapter, you'll use journaling to acknowledge the pain and start letting it go.

Exercise 1: The Memory Box

Think about the memories that still hold weight. Write about them, as fully as feels safe. Imagine locking those memories in a box inside you.

Prompt: What purpose do these memories serve in your life today?

____

____

____

____

____

____

____

____

____

____

____

____

Reflection Prompt: How do these memories shape how you see yourself today?

____

____

____

____

____

____

____

____

____

____

____

____

____

____

____

____

____

____

Exercise 2: Letting Go of Shame

Write down any shame you're holding onto, and challenge it. Replace it with more compassionate thoughts and perspectives.

____

____

____

____

____

____

____

____

____

____

____

____

____

____

Prompt: What would you say to someone else who feels this same shame?

____

____

____

____

____

____

____

____

____

____

____

____

____

____

Reflection Prompt: What would it feel like to let that shame go?

____

____

____

____

____

____

____

____

____

____

____

____

____

____

Exercise 3: Releasing the Journal

Write a letter to your past self, acknowledging the pain but also honoring your strength. Afterward, do a symbolic act of release—like tearing it up, burning it, or burying it.

____

____

____

____

____

____

____

____

____

____

____

____

____

____

Reflection Prompt: How did you feel after letting go of that letter?

CHAPTER 8

RELEASING THE PAST TO HEAL THE FUTURE

CHAPTER OBJECTIVE

To let go of past trauma and open up to
a hopeful future.

Healing isn't just about living in the present—it's about creating a future where your past doesn't hold power over you.

Reflection and Reframing:

Write a letter to your past self, acknowledging your strength. Release any guilt or shame you've been holding onto, and let go of the idea that your past will define your future.

____

____

____

CHAPTER 9

MOVING FORWARD WITH HOPE

CHAPTER OBJECTIVE

To envision a future where your past
no longer defines you.

Healing takes time, but it's important to envision a positive future. That vision is a powerful step in the healing process.

Reflection and Visioning:

Imagine a healed, empowered version of yourself. What does your life look like now? What kinds of relationships do you have?
Set one healing goal for the future and take one small step toward it today.

____
____
____
____
____
____
____
____
____
____
____
____
____
____
____
____
____
____
____
____
____
____
____

Affirmation for the Future

"I am worthy of love and respect."
"I am healing and reclaiming my power."
"I deserve a future filled with peace, joy, and empowerment."

CHAPTER 10

YOUR HEALING JOURNEY CONTINUES

CHAPTER OBJECTIVE

To reflect on your progress and celebrate
how far you've come.

Healing doesn't end—it's an ongoing journey. In this chapter, take a moment to acknowledge how far you've come, celebrate your progress, and give yourself grace when it's hard.

Reflection:

Look back at the steps you've taken. What have you learned about yourself? What practices have helped you most?

____
____
____
____
____
____
____
____
____
____
____
____
____
____
____
____
____
____
____
____
____
____

Final Thought:

You are worthy of love, respect, and joy. Keep moving forward, even on
the hard days. Every step is a victory.

*"Your healing is not a destination—it's a journey,
and you are doing amazing."*

Congratulations on completing this workbook! You have taken a courageous and transformative step toward healing and reclaiming your life. The journey you've embarked on is not easy, but every small step forward, every moment of self-compassion, and every piece of insight you've gained has helped you reconnect with your body, your mind, and your soul.

Healing is not a linear path—it's a journey with its ups and downs, its challenges and triumphs. But by facing your trauma with honesty and bravery, and by taking the time to nurture yourself, you are laying the foundation for a life filled with peace, joy, and empowerment. You are not defined by your past; you are defined by the strength you show today and the resilience you carry with you into the future.

Remember, you are worthy of love, respect, and healing. Your experiences do not diminish your worth—they only highlight the depth of your strength. As you move forward, continue to honor yourself, your body, and your emotions. Trust that each day brings new opportunities for growth, and that you have all the tools within you to navigate the future with confidence and grace.

You've already shown that you are capable of overcoming the most difficult of challenges, and now you have the power to create a future that is full of possibility. The work you've done here is just the beginning. Keep building on it. Keep seeking out the support you need, whether through therapy, self-care practices, or connecting with others who uplift you. Trust that you are worthy of all the healing, love, and joy that is coming your way.

Be proud of yourself for this journey. You are healing, you are growing, and you are reclaiming your power. And above all, you are not alone. You are part of a community of resilient, empowered individuals who are walking this path with you.

Your future is bright, and it's waiting for you.

With love, compassion, and belief in your strength,

Chioma Chime